KU-021-824

PEOPLE AND PLACES

BY MICHAEL CHINERY

CHERRYTREE BOOKS

A Cherrytree Book

Designed and produced by
A S Publishing

First published 2001
by Cherrytree Press
327 High Street
Slough
Berkshire
SL1 1TX

© Evans Brothers Limited 2001

All rights reserved. No part of this publication may be reproduced, stored in a
retrieval system or transmitted in any form or by any other means, electronic,
mechanical, photocopying or otherwise, without the prior permission of the
publishers.

British Library Cataloguing in Publication Data

Chinery, Michael
People and places. — (Secrets of the rainforest)
1. Rain forests — Juvenile literature
2. Rain forest people — Juvenile literature
I.Title
333.7'5

ISBN 1 842 34036 0

Design: Richard Rowan
Artwork: Malcolm Porter
Consultant: Sue Fogden

Printed in Hong Kong by Wing King Tong Co. Ltd

Acknowledgements
Photographs: *BBC Natural History Unit* Cover bottom &
back, 5 top, 6 top, 7, 8/9 top, 9, 10, 11 bottom, 12/13
top, 13 top, 14 bottom, 14/15 bottom, 15 top, 16,
17, 18 bottom, 19, 21 bottom, 22, 23, 24 top, 25
top, 26 top, 27 top right, 28/29 bottom; *Michael
Chinery* 5 bottom, 8 bottom, 18 top, 22/23
bottom; *Michael & Patricia Fogden* Cover top,
12 bottom, 21 top, 25 bottom, 26 bottom,
26 /27, 27, 28/29 top, 29; *Susan Fogden* 6/7
bottom, 11 top, 20, 20/21; *Nick
Gibbons* 4, 24 bottom, 28
bottom left; *David Harris* 14
top right.

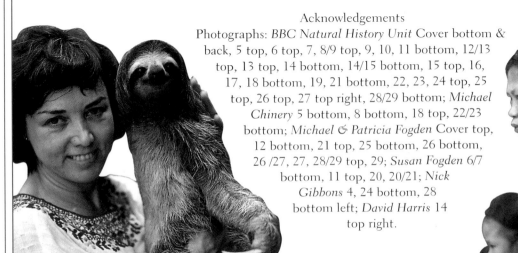

❖ CONTENTS ❖

☀ PEOPLE AND PLACES ☀

A S THE WORLD'S population
grows, more and more natural
habitats are destroyed to provide
land for homes and crops. Rainforests are
among the world's last remaining
wildernesses. The three main areas of
rainforest are in South America, Central
and West Africa, and Southeast Asia.
These areas are home to about 140
million people but, in the face of the
systematic destruction and settlement of
the forests, fewer and fewer of the
indigenous people are able to carry on
their traditional ways of life.

Fifty years ago the forests covered
twice as much land as they do today but
they have been remorselessly cut and
burned. Nearly 14 million hectares
disappear every year, an area about the
size of Greece.

TREES OF LIFE

Rainforests are home to many of the world's
tallest trees. There are also thousands of
smaller trees, sometimes more than 100
different kinds in a single hectare of forest,
and an incredible array of herbaceous plants.
Many of these scramble up the tree trunks
or grow perched on the branches high above
the ground. Not surprisingly, this rich and
varied vegetation teems with an equally rich
variety of animal – and
human – life.

▶ The map shows
how little primary,
or virgin,
rainforest
remains. When
small areas of
forests are cut
down, secondary
forest can regrow in
its place. If too much
forest is cut down, the forest
has no chance to recover.

NORTH AMERICA · EUROPE · ASIA · AFRICA · SOUTH AMERICA · AUSTRALIA
Tropic of Cancer · Equator · Tropic of Capricorn

Areas formerly covered by tropical rainforest
Areas of existing tropical rainforest

◀ Trees grow tall and strong in the rainforest. Their hard wood is so good for building and making furniture that many trees are now endangered species.

▲ These villagers live in the Congo rainforest in Africa. Most of the people farm small plots of land. Few live in the depths of the forest.

ROUND THE WORLD

RAINFORESTS, as their name suggests, grow in places with high rainfall. Tropical rainforests grow in a belt around the equator, bounded by the tropics of Cancer in the north and Capricorn in the south. In this region the average monthly temperature is above 25°C. In some of the forests closest to the equator it rains almost every day and over 600 cm of rain falls in a year. In these superwet forests trees stay green all through the year.

Forests further from the equator get slightly less rain with dry spells at certain times of the year. These include the monsoon forests of southern India and neighbouring countries. The trees are mostly evergreen but some are deciduous and drop their leaves in the drier season.

Rainforests do not grow only in the tropics. Some occur in cooler parts of the world, including the northern part of New Zealand and the western part of Tasmania (above). The important thing is that there must be lots of rain. Plant and animal life in these temperate rainforests is very different from that of the tropical rainforests. Many of the trees are conifers and there are also lots of tree ferns.

☼ PRECIOUS ENVIRONMENT ☼

BIOLOGISTS BELIEVE that more than half of the world's plant and animal species live in the tropical rainforests. No other habitat on earth supports such a wide variety of life. The Amazon rainforest, which is by far the largest remaining rainforest, exhibits a really amazing biodiversity. It shelters about 3,000 different kinds of birds, over one-third of the world's species. More than half of the world's freshwater fish live in the Amazon and its tributaries.

Many groups of people live in the rainforests. These indigenous people get all their food and medicines from the plants and animals. The plants also provide them with clothing and building materials. They use the rivers as hunting grounds and highways, and many build their homes by the water.

▶ Falling leaves decompose quickly in the hot, damp rainforest. Fungi and bacteria help to break them down and return their goodness to the soil.

◀ Villagers build communal longhouses alongside rivers in Southeast Asia. The houses are built entirely from rattans and other materials collected from the surrounding forest. The stilts keep them well above the water level.

▲ This Quechua hunter from the Amazon is pleased to have caught a parakeet with a dart from his blow gun. The bird's bright feathers may be used to make a colourful head-dress or other decoration. Nothing is wasted in the forest.

LAYERS OF LIFE

A rainforest contains several distinct habitats, each with its own kinds of plants and animals. The richest habitat is the sun-lit canopy of leafy branches that form the roof of the forest, usually about 30 metres above the ground. A number of even taller trees known as emergents push through the canopy here and there. Below the canopy is an understorey mainly of small trees that can stand plenty of shade.

Little light reaches the ground so few plants can survive on the forest floor, but armies of small animals join with fungi to dispose of the fallen leaves. The trunks of the large trees form yet another habitat. Plants called epiphytes perch on them and provide food and shelter for a wide range of insects and other creatures.

BY THE RIVER

Rivers form another important habitat. They teem with life, including freshwater dolphins, crocodiles and hundreds of strange fish. In many areas rivers flood at certain times of the year and the fish spread into the forest, feeding on fruits and seeds that fall into the water. Nearly one-tenth of Amazon trees rely on floods to disperse their seeds.

Along river banks, where light reaches the ground, there is a dense tangle of vegetation. Antelopes and other browsing animals live here rather than in the depths of the forest, where most of the foliage is out of their reach.

DESTRUCTION AND DEVASTATION

In the last 500 years, rainforest people, animals and plants have been under continuous pressure as so-called civilization has advanced into the wilderness. Millions of trees are cut down every year to provide timber, and millions more are cleared away for roads, farms, plantations and settlements. Mining and oil exploration have also destroyed large areas of rainforest in Africa and South America. In some parts of West Africa the only remaining areas of natural rainforest are small fragments that survive on slopes too steep for cultivation.

WHEN it rains in the forest, some of the water collects in streams and small ponds, providing fresh water for people and animals. The rest is soaked up by the roots and leaves of the great trees and the thirsty plants growing on them. In the heat of the sun, the leaves give off water in the form of vapour. Clouds form and rain falls again, and so the cycle continues day after day. Without the trees, the rain would wash into the rivers and run away to the sea. Gradually the land would dry up, and the people would have no fresh water.

◄ Rivers are the highways of the rainforests. Forest fruits and other products are for sale in this floating market in Thailand.

The destruction of the remaining rainforests would have wide-ranging effects. Forest-dwellers would lose their homes and their whole way of life. Many animals and plants would also become extinct, and with them many potentially valuable medicines and foods. People living around the forests would face devastating floods instead of secure supplies of safe drinking water, and climatic changes would be felt all over the world.

At last people are beginning to realize the importance of the rainforests and many organizations and governments are now working hard to prevent further destruction of this invaluable resource.

MANGROVE SWAMPS

AROUND many coasts and estuaries the tall trees of the rainforest give way to shorter trees called mangroves. These trees grow with their main roots under water. Many have special breathing roots that stick up from the mud. At low tide (right) these are exposed and can take in oxygen from the air. Mangrove swamps are important breeding grounds for fish, crabs and other animals that feed on the debris trapped around the roots. Birds gather to feed on the rich pickings. Many mangrove swamps are now in danger. They are being destroyed by land reclamation schemes in densely populated regions and by the establishment of fish farms.

● LIVING IN THE FORESTS ●

LIFE IN A rainforest is very different from life in a town or in the open countryside. Before settlers arrived and began to chop down the trees, ways of life in the forests had remained unchanged for thousands of years. People lived in harmony with nature, following the traditional ways of their ancestors. Some peoples, especially in the Amazon forest, still live in exactly this way, untouched by the changing world around them. Most others have been forced to change.

KNOWLEDGE AND RESPECT

Forest peoples mostly live in small nomadic or settled communities. Their traditions and customs ensure that they use the forest without harming it. Even hunters show respect and admiration for the animals they kill. The Ashwa people of Ecuador believe that every animal has some kind of spirit or magical power: the anaconda, for example, represents stealth, the jaguar bravery. Before setting out to hunt, the Ashwa ask these spirits to go with them and bring them success.

▼ Ashwa hunters use blowpipes and poison darts to catch swift-moving forest animals. Like most of the Ashwa this man has taken to wearing western clothes.

HUNTER-GATHERERS

SOME rainforest peoples, such as the Penan of Borneo and the Pygmies of Africa, are traditionally nomadic hunter-gatherers. They move through the forests and eat whatever they can find. Each family group occupies a territory of perhaps a few square miles, but rarely stays in any one spot for more than three or four days. Everyone is equal in these nomadic groups and there is no ruler or leader. All the food is shared and all the decisions are taken by the whole group. These Penan children (right) no longer follow the nomadic life. They live in longhouses provided by the government and probably know more about cartoon characters from comics than real animals in the forest.

Knowledge is handed down from parents to their children. Children learn to respect and admire the forest when they are young. They get to know all the trees and which plants to eat and which to use as medicines. They know precisely when certain trees will bear fruit, and learn all the tricks and skills for catching fish and other animals for food. Rainforest children do not have schools like ours: the forest is their school. They probably know much more about the wildlife around them than any scientist.

◄ Streams provide fresh water for drinking and bathing, and fish to eat. These Kayapo children will also quickly learn which plants are edible and which are poisonous.

SHIFTING CULTIVATION

Many forest peoples lead a more or less settled life. They live in larger communities and grow much of their food in small gardens around their homes. They choose an area of forest and clear it by cutting and burning the trees and shrubs, but leave the biggest and most admired trees in place. Then they till the soil and plant cassava, yams, sweet potatoes, maize, bananas, and various other crops.

The crops grow well for a few years, but soon use up all the nutrients in the soil. When the soil loses its fertility, the people abandon their garden and leave the forest to regrow. Meanwhile they clear another patch nearby. They return to the original site perhaps 10 years later when the soil has had a chance to recover. This system of shifting cultivation does no lasting harm to the forest – unlike large-scale agriculture.

BANANAS

Bananas are a source of carbohydrate and wealth. Big companies buy up the whole crop from poor farmers for low prices or grow them on

plantations where they pay low wages. They sell the bananas round the world for a big profit. These women from Senegal in Africa (above) probably grow enough to feed their families and sell a few by the roadside.

HAMBURGERS
. . . .

HAMBURGERS and beef products are popular in the United States but grazing land and labour are expensive. It is cheaper to clear rainforest land (left) in Central and South America. Because rainforest soils are so poor, even the pasture does not last long. Within ten years the cattle will have eaten all the thinning grass, leaving the exhausted soil exposed. With no trees left to provide seeds, there is no way that the forest can grow again. And, even if there were seeds, the soil is too poor for them to grow. Eventually the wind blows away the soil, leaving bare rock on land that was once thickly forested.

▲ Animals in the forest are at constant risk from poachers. This park warden in the Virunga National Park in Africa is removing a snare set to catch antelopes. The poachers can sell the skins, the meat and the horns.

BATTLE FOR SURVIVAL

Few rainforest people have not now had some contact with the outside world. A continuous stream of loggers, road-builders, miners, rubber planters, ranchers, scientists and missionaries have made their way into the forests, often with disastrous results for the inhabitants. Many have seen their homes and homelands disappear altogether.

Governments have resettled people in camps often far from their original homes. To live they have no choice but to work for the logging and mining companies or on the huge cattle ranches.

The foreign workers bring with them diseases, such as measles and influenza, to which the forest people have no immunity. Huge numbers die. During the last century as many as 90 groups of Amerindian peoples with separate cultures, languages and traditions died out in Brazil. Many more rainforest cultures will surely disappear if the people are not allowed to continue their traditional ways in undisturbed forests.

☀ PEOPLES OF THE AMAZON ☀

THE AMAZON rainforest covers an area of more than 500 million hectares. Hundreds of different peoples once lived in the forest, each with its own language and customs. Now only about 100 groups survive, totalling about 300,000 people. Forest cultures are fast disappearing as the people come into contact with settlers and adopt their habits. Many now wear manufactured clothes and use manufactured tools and weapons. These people are experts in forest management, but are now outnumbered by settlers bent on destroying it.

YANOMAMI

The Yanomami are the most numerous of the Amazon people still following something of their traditional lifestyle. About 20,000 Yanomami survive in huge protected areas of forest in Brazil and Venezuela. They live in small villages and practise shifting cultivation.

▼ Amazon children learn to respect nature. Though they hunt and eat monkeys, they also cherish them as pets.

▲ Raw cassava contains poison that has to be removed before it can be eaten. Women soak the chopped tubers and then squeeze the mush dry in tubular baskets. The poison runs away with the water.

▲ The Amazon is the biggest river in the world and it contains some big fish. In some places fishermen immerse stems from poisonous plants in the water. The poison drugs the fish and sends them to sleep, so that they are easily caught. The flesh is still safe to eat.

All the villagers usually live in one large longhouse called a *shabono*. The men hunt with blowpipes and bows and arrows and catch fish with arrows, harpoons and traps. The women cultivate crops on the land around their shabonos. As well as cassava, maize, sweet potatoes and paw-paws, they grow starchy bananas called plantains, which they cook before eating. Both men and women gather fruit, fungi and other wild foods from the forest.

The women also cultivate medicinal plants in their gardens and, although they do not need clothing in the hot climate, they grow cotton for making simple loin cloths and ornamental necklaces. They also paint their bodies with plant dyes, not just for decoration but for protection from insect bites.

◀ The easiest way to travel through the forest is by water. These hunters get everything they need from the forest: their scanty clothes, their bows and arrows and even the canoe.

LOGGERS AND MINERS

Since the 1600s the Yanomami have been under threat from outsiders keen to exploit the Amazon's wealth: its trees, its gold, its precious stones and the land itself. In the last hundred years, loggers, miners and road-builders have invaded Yanomami homelands, enslaving the people or killing those who tried to resist. Many more died from pollution and disease. Perhaps a quarter of all Yanomami perished and they are not entirely safe today, even though they live on protected reserves. Gold and other metals are worth a lot of money and speculators and mining companies continue to exploit the Yanomami lands, especially in Brazil.

KAYAPO

The Kayapo people live around the Xingu river in southern Amazonia. They hunt and fish with bows and arrows and blowpipes, and gather all kinds of fruits and fungi from the forest, but they also grow much of their food. Cassava and maize are their main crops, together with 14 different varieties of banana and many other edible and medicinal plants brought in from the forest. The Kayapo know exactly what sort of plants to grow on each kind of soil and how to find and kill different animals. They use compost to enrich their gardens and biological controls for pests. They avoid damage by leaf-cutter ants, for example, by bringing in another kind of ant whose smell keeps the leaf-cutters away.

OIL AND THE WAORANI

THE Waorani and other forest peoples of Ecuador, on the western edge of Amazonia, had probably never seen an outsider until the 1950s. Until that time they had no metal and made do with simple stone tools. They lived mainly by hunting and gathering, and occasionally growing crops. The men and boys were agile tree-climbers, and their forest life made them strong and healthy. But prospectors found oil on their lands and now there are wells and pipelines where the trees once stood. Many Waorani took jobs with the oil companies that had destroyed their homes and way of life. Today only a few hundred Waorani survive. Other people, like this Ashwa family (left), have been uprooted from their homeland along with the trees. The Kofan people of the forest (above) have no cars and no use for oil. Though it was found on their territory, they do not share in the profits made from it.

SETTLERS FROM THE NORTH

THE indigenous people of South and Central America are known as Amerindians. They arrived in several waves from North America about 15,000 years ago and brought maize and several other crops with them. They gradually spread all over South America. Many took up residence in the rainforests, where each group settled in a particular area and developed its own language and culture. This boy is from the ancient Maya culture of Mexico.

▲ This Kayapo craftsman is just starting another head-dress like the one he is wearing, which is made of macaw feathers.

Much of the Kayapo forest homeland has been destroyed during the last 20 years, mostly by illegal mining. The Kayapo, who have a reputation for fierceness, have tried to defend their lands, but the miners are too wealthy and too powerful. A greater threat looms in the shape of dams being built on the Xingu river to provide hydroelectricity for industries and homes thousands of miles away. They will cause flooding of thousands of hectares of Kayapo land.

◀ Many displaced forest people have no choice but to work in mines. The rainforest that once covered this open-cast tin mine in Brazil will not regrow when the tin is exhausted. The land will be barren.

PEOPLES OF AFRICAN RAINFORESTS

BECAUSE OF the demand for timber and for agricultural land, the once lush rainforests of West Africa have virtually disappeared during the last few decades. A few upland areas remain in Cameroon and shelter many birds that are found nowhere else in the world, but elsewhere most of the forest has been cleared. It has been replaced by cocoa and oil palm plantations. The indigenous people now live in settlements or on the outskirts of towns. Some work on plantations but jobs are scarce. Those without work may grow a few cash crops for sale in local markets or to tourists.

PYGMIES

More rainforest survives in Central Africa, in the basin of the vast Congo river. The best known of the indigenous people are Pygmies, but only a few thousand of them remain. They belong to several groups, including the Bambuti, the Baka, and the Efe, and they live almost entirely by hunting and gathering. They use bows and arrows and nets to catch animals, and also eat lots of insects, including juicy caterpillars and beetle grubs. The children learn to distinguish the poisonous ones from the edible ones at an early age.

Honey is also an important food and the men climb high into the trees to collect it from bees' nests. They are skilled climbers and link the tree-tops together with bridges made from twisted vines or lianas.

▲ These West African people try to make money by selling fruit to tourists.

▶ Pygmies are fearless climbers. This man is climbing down with a leafy basket full of honeycomb.

▼ The decorations on the faces of these Bambuti Pygmies are mainly for ceremonial purposes now, but may originally have helped to camouflage hunters.

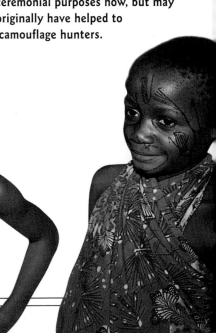

▲ Pygmies make nets from plant fibres and use them for catching animals and carrying loads. They carry heavy items on their heads.

The Pygmies live in small communities of perhaps 20 to 30 households and are always on the move. They build simple huts with branches and leaves, but rarely stay in any one hut for more than a few days. They frequently trade with farming communities outside the forest, offering meat, fish, and medicinal herbs in return for cloth, fruit and tools, such as axes and saws.

SHORT AND NIMBLE

The Pygmy people are rarely more than one-and-a-half metres tall. Their small size has probably evolved over thousands of years as an adaptation to forest life. Small people can climb trees more quickly and easily than larger people. They can also move more quietly through tangled riverside vegetation.

GREAT AFRICAN APES

CHIMPANZEES (right) are our nearest living relatives. They live in family bands and travel through the shrinking forests in search of food. Despite conservation measures, they are hunted for food or for sale as pets. The pygmy chimpanzee, or bonobo, may be in danger of extinction. Nobody knows how many are left. Gorillas, too, are in danger. Mountain gorillas have recently become victims of war, killed by mines or soldiers. The best hope for these creatures is peace and tourism. If local people can earn money by showing them to visitors, it will be in their interest to conserve them.

● PEOPLES OF ASIAN RAINFORESTS ●

T HE FORESTS of Southeast Asia have suffered more from logging than any other area of rainforest. Large areas of rainforest remain only on the islands of Borneo and New Guinea. Numerous groups of indigenous people still follow their traditional hunting and gathering lives in these forests. New Guinea probably has over 300 such peoples, each with its own language. Some live in such remote areas that they were unknown to outsiders until the 1970s.

THE PENAN OF SARAWAK

The Penan, or Punan, people of Sarawak on the island of Borneo lived as nomadic hunters and gatherers, but most of their forests have now been destroyed to feed the timber trade. Fewer than 7,000 Penan people exist today, and only about 300 of them continue their nomadic existence, living in temporary shelters built with poles tied together with rattans and roofed with palm leaves. These surviving nomads live freely in the Gunung Mulu National Park, where they continue to extract sago from palms, feast on ripe mangoes and hunt wild pigs.

The rest of the Penan have been resettled in camps where, instead of living in individual huts, they share communal longhouses like those of their rice-growing

▼ Sago is the pith of a palm tree. The women chop it, soak it and tread it to reduce it to a pulp that dries as flour that can be used in cooking. Rather than harvesting and preparing their own sago, most Penan now buy commercially produced flour.

RICE GROWERS

. . . .

T HE Dayaks and several other peoples in Borneo are farmers known as longhouse people. They live together in huts (above) that house up to 100 families, each with its own quarters. The whole structure is built of poles lashed together with rattan. The houses are built on stilts to protect the people from floods and wild animals. The peoples' main crop is rice,

ENDANGERED ORANGS

ORANG-UTANS are among
the many animals of
Southeast Asia endangered by
the destruction of the rainforests.
They still survive in Sumatra and
Borneo and they are legally
protected, but they are being
squeezed into ever smaller areas.
Poachers still catch the babies for
the pet trade, often killing the
mothers to get hold of them.
Conservationists try to rescue the
captive orangs and retrain them
for life in the forest.

and its cultivation is central to
all their activities. They perform
special rituals during the sowing
and growing seasons to secure a
good crop. They also grow fruit
and vegetables and medicinal
plants in small forest clearings.
The men and boys hunt in what
remains of the forest, and earn a
small income from
selling meat
and timber.

◀ A Penan mother with her baby. His
carrier is skilfully made from
bark and rattan, and can be
used for carrying other
loads. When the time
comes, his children will
probably have a mass-
produced plastic carrier.

neighbours. Away from the forest and unused to growing
food, they have a poor quality of life. Many now work for the
logging companies, but some still trek back to the forest to
hunt. They bring back meat to eat and sell to the loggers or
to exchange for clothes.

Although these Penan people survive, their culture is
disappearing. The children cannot learn the skills and
freedom of forest life, and there are few schools for them to
learn about the modern world. The Bateq of Malaysia and
the Kubu of Sumatra are also fast disappearing with fewer
than 2,000 individuals at present.

HOME IN THE TREES

In the centre of New Guinea, on the steep forested slopes of
the mountains, live several groups of warlike hunter-
gatherers who traditionally made their homes high in the
trees. They include the Korowai and the Kombai, whose
flimsy-looking tree houses were as much as 50 metres off the
ground. Such homes were
more easily defended than
homes on the ground. Some
families are now building
homes at lower levels. They
hunt with bows and arrows,
but their main source of
food is sago.

FORESTS UNDER THREAT

DESPITE THE warnings of conservationists and other scientists, many of the remaining areas of rainforest are still in danger from the world's expanding human population. Even those in national parks and other protected areas are being eroded at the edges as people move in and cut down the trees. Hundreds of animals, including orang-utans, macaws and many monkeys, have become rare. Hundreds more have become extinct as their homes have been destroyed.

CHANGING LIVES

Many of the indigenous people have also disappeared. When Portuguese settlers first arrived in Brazil about 500 years ago there were

▼ A road slices through the Amazon forest in northern Brazil. The Nambiquara people were almost wiped out when a road was built through their territory because the workers brought so many diseases with them.

CUTTING DOWN TREES

LOGS from the Indian rainforest (above) await transport to the timber factory. Timber has always been taken from the rainforests for fuel or for building or making furniture. For a long time the forests were treated like mines, with enormous quantities of timber being taken out and nothing put back – so the forests quickly shrank. Today, conservationists try to ensure that all timber comes from renewable resources – either from plantations or from well-managed forests where every tree cut down is replaced with a young one for the future. But not all governments are concerned with conservation.

WARFARE

Wars in Central Africa have affected the people and animals of the rainforests. People uprooted by the fighting have been forced to live off the land. Hutu refugees fleeing from the civil war in Ruanda in the 1990s moved into the neighbouring Democratic Republic of Congo and started to cut down the forests for fuel (left) at a rate of 900 tonnes a day. Gorillas in and around Ruanda were also affected by the war. Some were killed in the fighting and others were driven from their homes by the influx of refugees. But the animals are now protected and should be safe, as tourists return to the area and help pay for their conservation.

▼ Many people in Southeast Asia live close to starvation. Rice-fields can feed more people than rainforests and the people need wood from the forests for fuel.

probably about five million Amerindians in the country, most of whom lived in the rainforest. Today there are fewer than 300,000, and most do not live in the forest.

Of the few rainforest peoples who do maintain their traditional ways of life almost all have had their lives changed in some way by contact with the outside world. Many now wear manufactured clothes, for example, and use guns instead of blowpipes or bows and arrows. Other forest people have had their lives changed completely. Forced to leave their shrinking forest homes, they now live in camps or settlements set up by governments. Although the governments want them to integrate with the rest of the population, the people are often unhappy and unable to adapt to their new unnatural lives.

► This huge dam will provide electricity for the ever-growing cities of Brazil. The people and animals that lived in the vast area of forest covered by the lake lost their homes.

FROM FOREST TO FARM

The conversion of forest to farmland continues in all rainforest areas. By the 1980s, about a quarter of the Central American rainforest had been turned to cattle pasture to satisfy the demand for cheap beef in the United States. But the pastures were generally of poor quality and many have now been abandoned. Much of the land would have been better used to grow crops for local people to eat. Much of West Africa's rainforest has also been replaced by poor-quality farmland or by cocoa and oil palm plantations. The rainforests of Southeast Asia have been replaced by extensive rice-fields and by plantations of rubber trees and oil palms.

ROADS TO RUIN

Plantations, mines and logging companies all need roads to get people and equipment into the forest and their products out. Roads are also necessary to link countries and cities. But roads cause problems. As well as destroying trees and driving people from their homes, they allow newcomers to settle in the forest. Often

▼ A roadside village in Cameroon, West Africa, where conservationists are working with local farmers to increase the productivity of the land. This will reduce the need to encroach further into the remaining forest, which is home to many rare birds.

MAKING WAY FOR MINES

SEEN from the air this gold-mining area in the Brazilian rainforest (left) is an ugly scar. The land may also have been poisoned by mercury, used to separate the gold from other metals. Brazil probably has the world's largest deposits of iron ore under its rainforest, and also has gold deposits that attract large numbers of prospectors and miners. Huge coal deposits lie underneath the rainforests of New Guinea, and there are vast reserves of oil in Venezuela, Nigeria and Ecuador. Mining and drilling for these minerals have already destroyed or polluted large areas of rainforest and driven many indigenous people from their homes. It is not just the areas close to the mines or wells that have been destroyed: enormous stretches of forest have been cut down to make way for roads and to provide fuel for smelters and other industrial plants.

RAGING FIRES

FIRE is a fast and cheap way of clearing the forest. Every day thousands of hectares are deliberately set on fire to clear the debris after the larger trees have been removed. The ash helps to fertilize the soil, although its minerals are soon used up. Uncontrolled fires can burn for a long time and destroy an immense area of forest and its wildlife. This happened in Indonesia in 1997, when the normally short dry season dragged on. Smoke from fires all over the country blotted out the sun for hundreds of miles and caused health and pollution problems in neighbouring countries. Parts of the Brazilian rainforest have also been badly damaged by fires. This area (above) has been cleared for cattle ranching.

encouraged or even forced by governments to move from overcrowded towns, the settlers establish overcrowded roadside villages. They clear the nearby forest by slash-and-burn and grow cash crops. Without fertilizers the soil is soon exhausted, so the settlers move further into the forest and start again. They have no experience of shifting cultivation and do not recognize the signs of soil exhaustion until it is too late for the forest to recover.

◄ Jaguars once roamed the forests of South and Central America but now their habitat has shrunk. They are hunted for their skins and by farmers who kill them to protect their livestock.

❂ HOPE FOR THE FORESTS ❂

MOST OF THE world's rainforests are in poor countries where neither individuals nor governments have money for conservation. The trees are a resource that they need for building and fuel and that they can export to earn money from abroad. They cannot afford to protect the forests, so people and governments from rich countries must do so. Many countries and organizations give money in return for assurances that the forests will be preserved. They provide money for the management of national parks, for training park rangers and for scientific studies. Any scheme for safeguarding the rainforests must involve the indigenous people and make their needs a priority. They can teach conservationists the best way to preserve the forests, because they have preserved them for generations. They may also help scientists find medicines that will be useful to the whole world.

▶ Angry at the invasion and destruction of their homeland, these Quechua people from Ecuador are protesting about a new oil development by blocking the access road.

A CLOSER LOOK

UNTIL recently the canopy was virtually out of reach to scientists. Only by studying freshly fallen trees or by peering up with binoculars could they get much idea of the richness of life high above their heads. Modern techniques and materials now make it possible to get up into the canopy and examine plant and animal life at close range. Researchers have discovered thousands of new species, including tiny mice, that live permanently in the tree-tops. As well as looking for species that will benefit the wider world, they study how the plants and animals live and what their particular needs are. By studying the habits and needs of rainforest species, scientists can evaluate the best ways of conserving their habitat. This researcher (left) is holding a baby three-toed sloth.

▼ ▲ To reach the canopy, a researcher first fires a fishing line over a high branch. She uses the line to haul up a stouter line, and then a proper climbing rope.

With feet and hands firmly fixed into ratchet devices, she can 'walk' up the rope in complete safety.

PEOPLE FIRST

All round the world, the peoples of the rainforest have suffered inhuman treatment from meddling settlers, missionaries, governments and businesses. Their land has been stolen from them and their way of life has been wiped out. After centuries of subjugation, forest people are beginning to fight for their rights and demand land and security, and governments are beginning to take notice of them.

In 1997 the Brazilian government created 22 new reservations for its indigenous peoples, covering an area of over 30,000 square miles, about the size of Scotland. Altogether, they have rights to more than one-tenth of the country's territory. The land is not all rainforest and it is not owned by the people, but they have a guaranteed right to live there.

Despite this, their forest homeland is not entirely safe. Illegal mining and logging will always occur because the areas are too big to guard effectively. The people themselves, having seen the financial rewards obtained by some of the farmers and miners, also want to exploit the land and mineral reserves. Convincing them that short-term gains will destroy the forest and their homeland forever is a job for scientists and conservationists. Only when the people are persuaded that a better and more profitable living can be obtained from properly managed forests will the rainforests be safe.

▲ Lightweight sectional towers like this help scientists study the canopy.

NATIONAL PARKS AND TOURISM

One way for the people of the forests to earn money is to show the splendours of the forests to outsiders. Tourism generates a huge amount of money for conservation and for the local people. It encourages them to look after the forests because it is in their best interests to do so. Birdlife International is one organization involved with several rainforest conservation projects. It works with governments to make local people aware of the long-term value of their remaining forests. Conservationists and forest-users are finding ways of continuing to take food and fuel from the forest without destroying it. Project workers also help people to make the surrounding farmland more productive, thereby reducing their need to encroach further into the remaining forest.

PACHAMAMA

Young people throughout the world are helping to save the forests because they know that the forests are vital to the world. *Pachamama* is the word for 'mother earth' in the language of the ancient Inca people of Peru. The rainforests are the earth's lungs. Without them, our mother earth may wither and die. If you want to help, it is easy to join a conservation organization. You can become involved with interesting projects that will help to save the forests and our mother earth.

▼ These youngsters are helping scientists to catch and ring birds in the forest in Cameroon, West Africa.

INSECTS GALORE!

BIOLOGISTS study insect life in the canopy by spraying small areas with a mist of quick-acting insecticide. This technique is known as fogging. The affected insects fall on to sheets on the ground below and can be gathered up and inspected. The results have been astounding. For example, over 1,200 different species of beetles have been collected from the

▼ Local people can earn money from tourists, who love to buy goods like this pot being painted by a Zapora woman in Ecuador.

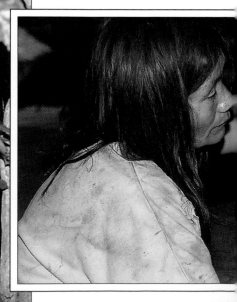

canopy of just one kind of tree
in Panama. Figures like this have
made biologists revise their
estimates of the numbers of
insect species on earth. Instead
of two or three million, some
biologists now think there could
be as many as 15 or even 30
million. The insecticide used in
these studies quickly breaks
down and does no long-term
damage to the forest. This insect
(above) is a bush cricket from
Malaysia.

▶ Tourists admire a waterfall in a
national park in Costa Rica. Too many
tourists could harm the rainforests, so
forest managers limit the numbers.

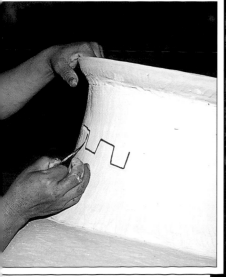

❋ GLOSSARY ❋

Amerindian Another name for Native American people, especially those of South America.

Bacteria Microscopic forms of life that exist everywhere in nature and play an important part in the breakdown and recycling of dead plants and animals. Many of them, often known as germs, cause disease in living plants and animals.

Biodiversity The variety of species found in any natural region. The rainforests contain more species than any other habitat.

Biological control The use of one kind of animal to control another that has become a pest.

Blowpipe A narrow tube, usually some kind of hollow stem, used for firing darts or pellets at prey.

Canopy The 'roof' of the rainforest, formed by the leafy branches of the trees.

Carbohydrate Any kind of food material consisting of just carbon, hydrogen and oxygen. Starch and sugar are good examples. Carbohydrates provide energy.

Cash crop A crop grown for sale rather than for home consumption.

Compost A mass of rotted or partly rotten leaves and other vegetation used as fertilizer to encourage the growth of plants.

Conifer Any plant that carries its pollen and seeds in cones. Most conifers are large trees and most of them are evergreen.

Conservation The scientific management of a natural habitat, such as a rainforest, designed to ensure the survival of the maximum possible numbers of plant and animal species.

Debris A collection of fragments of plant, animal or mineral origin.

Deciduous tree Any tree that drops all of its leaves for part of the year.

Emergent Any large tree that grows above the rainforest canopy.

Epiphyte Any plant that grows on another, especially on the branches of a tree, but takes no food from it. Ferns, orchids and bromeliads are common epiphytes in the rainforests.

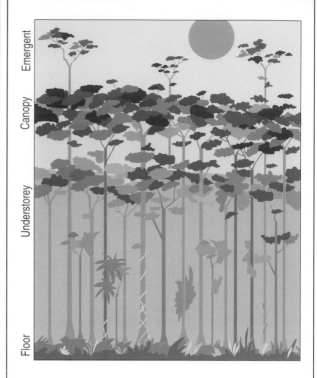

▲ A rainforest has layers of vegetation. Low shrubs grow on the forest floor, and slender young trees form an understorey below the vast, dense canopy of tree-tops. At intervals taller trees called emergents poke their heads through the canopy. All the plants are trying to get a share of the sunlight.

Equator The imaginary line around the centre of the earth, midway between the north and south poles.

Extinct An animal or plant species is said to be extinct when it has no living representatives.

Fertility A measure of the soil's ability to support crops or other plants.

Fertilizer Any substance or mixture of materials added to the soil to promote plant growth.

Fungi A group of plant-like organisms that lack the green pigment chlorophyll and are therefore unable to make their own food. They feed by absorbing nutrients from other living or dead plants or animals. The group includes mushrooms and moulds.

Herbaceous plant Any non-woody plant.

Indigenous Native to or occurring naturally in a particular area.

Land reclamation The process of converting swamps and other wet areas into dry land.

ENDANGERED!

●●●●●●●●●●●●●●●●●●●●●●●●●●●●●●●●●●●

RAINFORESTS are vitally important to the well-being of the world but they are in danger of destruction. Many of the animals and plants featured in this book are under threat from forest clearance. If you are interested in knowing more about rainforests and in helping to conserve them, you may find these addresses and websites useful.

Worldwide Fund for Nature
 WWF (Australia), *Level 5, 725 George Street, Sydney, NSW 2000*
 WWF (South Africa), *116 Dorp Street, Stellenbosch 7600*
 WWF (UK), *Panda House, Weyside Park, Cattershall Lane, Godalming, Surrey GU17 1XR*

Rainforest Foundation,
A5 City Cloisters, 188-96 Old St, London EC1V 9FR

Friends of the Earth, Rainforest Campaign, *26-28 Underwood Street, London N1 7JQ*

Worldwide Fund for Nature
http://www.wwf-uk.org

Friends of the Earth
http://www.foe.co.uk

Environmental Education Network
http://envirolink.org.enviroed/

Rainforest Foundation
http://rainforestfoundationuk.org

Rainforest Preservation Foundation
http://www.flash.net/~rpf/

Survival International
http://www.survival.org.uk

Sustainable Development
http://iisd1.iisd.ca/

Rainforest Action Network
http://www.igc.apc.org/ran/intro.html

Liana A climbing plant with long, woody stems that hang from the trees like ropes. Also known as lianes or vines, lianas belong to many different plant families.

Longhouse Name given to a long building, often on stilts, that houses several or many families.

Mangrove Any of a group of small, evergreen trees with tangled, basket-like roots that grow around tropical coasts.

Monsoon forest A tropical forest with a marked dry season of varying length.

Nomadic Roaming from place to place, with no fixed home.

Nutrient Any of the essential food materials needed by plants or animals.

Plantation An area that has been cleared and planted with cash crops, especially trees or shrubs.

Pollute To contaminate the air, land or water with harmful substances.

Primary forest Forest that has never been cut; also called virgin forest.

Rattan One of a number of climbing palms whose flexible stems are widely used for building shelters in the rainforest and for making cane furniture.

Renewable resource A source of food, fuel or other material that can be renewed regularly by replacing what people remove. Properly managed forests are renewable resources because trees are always planted to replace those that are cut down.

Secondary forest Forest that has developed in areas where the original or primary forest has been destroyed.

Shabonos Name given to the communal houses of the Yanomami people in the Amazon.

Shifting cultivation A system of agriculture in which people cultivate small areas of land for a few years and then move to new areas.

Slash-and-burn A method of clearing the forest by cutting down the trees and then burning them. The ashes help fertilize the soil.

Superwet forest A rainforest close to the equator where rainfall is particularly heavy.

Temperate rainforest Any rainforest growing in the cooler parts of the world, outside the tropics.

Tropics Parts of the world, on each side of the equator, where the climate is hot all year.

Understorey The layer of vegetation, consisting mainly of young trees, growing well below the level of the canopy.

Virgin forest Forest that has never been cut; also called primary forest.

❂ INDEX ❂